The Rhythm of the Seasons

NATURE-INSPIRED AFFIRMATIONS FOR REST, GROWTH, AND RENEWAL

ARDEN LANE

Copyright © 2026 by Arden Lane
All rights reserved.
No part of this book may be reproduced, stored in a retrieval system, or transmitted in any form or by any means, electronic or mechanical, including photocopying, recording, or otherwise, without prior written permission from the publisher, except in the case of brief quotations used in reviews or other noncommercial uses permitted by law.
Artwork and Imagery
All watercolor sketches appearing in this book were created by the author.
Photographic images are a combination of original works and licensed imagery obtained from professional image libraries and design resources. All images are used in accordance with applicable licensing agreements.
Publisher Imprint
Published by Voyage & Quill
An imprint of Voyage & Quill Publishing
This book is a work of reflection and inspiration. It is not intended as medical, psychological, or professional advice.
First edition
ISBN: 978-1-918385-25-0

entering the
RHYTHM

This book is an invitation to slow your steps and soften your gaze.

Nature does not hurry. It unfolds. It rests. It returns. Every leaf, every tide, every season moves according to a rhythm older than memory. When we pause long enough to notice, that rhythm begins to echo within us.

We are taught to measure time in deadlines and distance, yet the earth keeps time differently. It grows when it is ready. It sheds when it must. It rests without apology. There is wisdom in this quiet certainty, in the knowing that nothing blooms forever and nothing remains dormant without purpose.

These pages are not meant to be read quickly. They are meant to be opened slowly, returned to often, and held gently. Let the words meet you where you are. Let the images remind you of what you already know but may have forgotten.
You may find yourself drawn to a single line and stay there for a while. You may move through a season out of order. You may come back months later and read the same words differently. This is part of the rhythm.

As the year turns, so do we. There are times for becoming, times for expanding, times for releasing, and times for resting. Each phase carries its own quiet beauty. Each one asks for something different from us.

May this book be a companion through those cycles. A place to return to when the world feels loud. A reminder that you are allowed to move at a natural pace. A reflection of the steady, patient unfolding that exists both around you and within you.

Step in gently.
The rhythm is already waiting.

A rhythm exists beneath all things,
patient and steady,
waiting to be noticed.

This book was created to be met gently.

You may choose to move through it with the seasons, letting each chapter accompany the natural shifts of the year. Spring when you are beginning again. Summer when life feels full. Autumn when you are ready to release. Winter when rest and reflection call.

You may also open this book intuitively. Let your hands choose the page. Trust that the words you land on are the ones meant to meet you in that moment. Some readers return to this book as a quiet ritual.

A single page in the morning to set the tone for the day. One affirmation in the evening to soften the edges of what has passed. There is no need to read more than one. Let the words settle. Let the image breathe.

This book is also an offering. A companion gifted with care. A reminder that growth is not linear, rest is necessary, and every season holds its own wisdom.

There is no right way to use this book.

Only the way that feels true to you.

Spring:
BECOMING

Something begins
before you are ready.

A soft insistence
beneath the surface.

You do not need proof.
You do not need speed.

What is growing
knows its own timing.

Let it begin quietly.

I allow myself to begin gently.

Something new is forming, even if I cannot yet name it.

I step forward with calm courage.
I allow myself to become.

I trust small beginnings to carry quiet strength.

I am allowed to start again without explanation.

What is unfolding within me has its own timing.

I nurture what is just beginning.
I release the need to be ready.

I soften into change rather than resist it.

honor progress that happens beneath the surface.

Hope returns in subtle ways.

I listen to what is asking to grow.

I meet this season with openness and care.

Becoming does not require certainty.

I give myself permission to grow slowly.

New possibilities are allowed to arrive quietly.

I am learning to move with patience.

I welcome change as a gentle invitation.

Each step forward is enough.
I trust the process, even when the
outcome is unclear.

There is space for renewal in my life.

My beginnings are worthy of care.

Summer
EXPANDING

A rhythm exists
beneath all things,
patient and steady,
waiting to be noticed.

I allow myself to take up space.

I trust the fullness of this moment.

I trust my capacity to hold more.

I am present in my body and my life.

Joy is allowed to arrive without explanation.

I receive what is offered with ease.

I am comfortable being seen.

I stand comfortably in who I am becoming.

I let abundance meet me where I am.

I move through the world
with quiet confidence.

I let life feel generous.

I honor the strength of what
I have grown.

I give myself permission to enjoy this season.

I am grounded, open,
and fully here.

I move with ease and intention.

I trust myself in moments of expansion.

I welcome vitality into my days.

I belong in experiences that feel

I inhabit my life fully.

I allow warmth to soften me.

Things fall
not to be lost,
but to return to the earth
that held them first.

What has given its season
is complete.

There is grace
in the letting go.

Rest waits quietly
beneath it all.

I release what has finished its work.

I honor what this season has given me.

I welcome the calm that follows release.

Letting go makes room for rest.

I trust the natural rhythm of endings

I find beauty in what is passing.

I allow myself to rest from becoming.

Gratitude softens every release.

I no longer carry what
no longer serves me

I allow change to be gentle.

I honor the turning of the season within me.

I acknowledge all that has been lived.

I prepare inwardly with care.

What I release returns to
the earth in its own way.

I recognize when it is time to lay something down.

I make space for quiet reflection.

There is peace in allowing things to complete.

I hold gratitude for every chapter.

Nothing needs to be held forever.

I loosen my grip with trust.

Nothing asks you
to move right now.

Beneath the stillness,
life is listening.

Roots hold fast
in the dark.

Rest is not an ending.
It is a gathering.

Stay awhile.

I allow myself to rest without guilt.

Stillness is supporting me.

I am resilient, even at rest.

I trust the strength that grows quietly.

Nothing needs to be proven right now.

I honor the wisdom of slowing down.

I listen inwardly with patience.

Rest is part of my becoming.

I am held, even in stillness.

What is unseen is still alive.

I rest, knowing renewal will come.

I conserve my energy with care.

Silence nourishes me.

I trust what is taking shape beneath the surface.

This season asks nothing more of me.

I do not rush what is meant to unfold slowly.

Solitude restores me.

I allow myself to pause completely.

I gather myself gently.

Quiet strengthens me.

www.ingramcontent.com/pod-product-compliance
Lightning Source LLC
Chambersburg PA
CBHW061124070526
44584CB00033B/4214